LIGHTFALLS

Gillie Robic

LIVE CANON

First Published in 2019
By Live Canon Ltd
www.livecanon.co.uk

978-1-909703-79-7

LIGHTFALLS

Gillie Robic was born in India, an abiding love and influence, and lives in London. She attended the Sorbonne and UCAD in Paris, and the Central School of Art in London. She is a poet, voice artist and puppeteer, currently designing and directing a puppet production of an ancient Indian epic. Gillie is now happily drowning in poetry. Her poems have appeared in magazines and anthologies in the UK and the US. She has won, or been placed in, several competitions. Her first collection, *Swimming Through Marble*, was shortlisted and published in 2016 by Live Canon. This is her second collection.

Acknowledgements

The following poems have previously appeared in the following publications: 'Listen, St Michael', *South Magazine*; 'In the End', 'Old Vines', *South Bank Poetry*; 'Muscle', *The Hippocrates Book of the Heart*, Hippocrates Press.

Special thanks

to Elizabeth Horsley, Geoff Lander and Michel Robic, who very wonderfully read the manuscript and nudged me in the light direction.

Contents

PART III: Worry Beads

For Pamela

PART I

Broken Angels

godforsaken

I sometimes meet the devil
at unexpected moments.
I know him by his finger
underwriting darkness,
scribbling on the light of god,
most desolate when striving
to pinch out his own flame.

Listen, St Michael

I don't want to be an angel,
it hurts so much to pluck out the telltale feathers.
The down is just embarrassing,
but it's the quills that are the worst.
If I try and hide them under my shirt
I look like some old dosser,
clothes stuffed against the cold.

It's all right for you, Michael,
Taxiarch Archangel, Chief of the armies of God.
You lived in interesting times,
went up against Satan and won.
Ever since, Great Art has depicted you
all toned muscles and graceful stance,
you never even look out of breath.

Me, I just want to live a normal life,
have a good time, earn my crust,
down a few jars at the weekend and get laid.
I can't remember most of what I do
but my mates are with me and they grin.
Come Monday morning there are more effing feathers
prickling my shoulder blades. It's vexatious.

Anyway, how can I put a stop to it?
I don't have time to wax my back – and this headache!
Well, it's like a ring of hot metal round my head.
I can't sleep, there seems to be light everywhere.
My concentration's shot, my work is suffering.
All I do is rock back and forth moaning
Oh God! Oh God! Oh God!

marginalia

small thing on the rim
visible only when light catches it

how everyday imperatives intrude

it's easier to wander round the edges
where notional gridlines become visible
but mean nothing

unable to see beyond this
wall
no idea which side is

ear pressed to the bricks for clues
because here is not the centre and maybe
there's nothing further than

still feeling the way
towards
whatever light there is to catch

Castoff

Step out of your demon skin,
let it puddle around your ankles.
Balance like a Botticelli vision
on the edge of your own pink shell,
a peeled prawn on a good hair day.

You want so much to be good and loved.
Why else would you stand naked
and winsome? You don't do winsome.
Already the effort colours your cheeks
and presses on your coccyx.

Your overpainted reputation is cracking
through the pigment.
Your role is to be the bad guy,
scapegoat for the wonky stars.
Circumvent your karma,

bring people together, even dodgily.
Keep everything anxious, on the edge.
Pry contented away from smug.
Spread darkness so we search for light.
Pray for somebody to hold you out of fear.

Irretrievable

I set up my angels,
demons knock them over in play.
Of all the broken pieces
some burnish, some crack my heart.

Broken angels are my coat of dust,
demons warm my hands;
fallen from the pinioned host,
they ache to make amends.

Tableau: lovers in a garden,
feathered serpents asleep in the trees,
fermenting apples on the altar,
honey on the knife.

Not on the moon in any way

She lies, a woman with her voice cut,
straddled by a seeming angel
ministering, or sucking blood.
Wings of silk, gemstone eyes bleeding,
face suffused with sorrow.

Behind him the boy brays
through huge yellow teeth,
stamping the earth, searching
for somewhere to plant his hooves.

I remember how he knelt
me on the riverbank,
knocking over the bait box in his hurry,
catching the bottle as it fell.

I cried, scratched his ears,
not with affection.

His back opens and opens,
spews damp grey pinions
over my nakedness.

As they dry they lift, blur,
vector us out of the dark.

A sea of tranquility stretches
flat under unbiased stars,
where sound-waves end
and the boy dissolves.

silver donkeys

road silvers
through night
wobbles air
residual heat
silver donkeys
wobble road
light-footed
no load
silver spinning
mirrored light
moon at full
transfigures sight
impartial space
cradles all
eagles' flight
angels' fall

Jacob's Ladder

My house is filled with cumulus.
I crouch outside
gripping the balustrade, gaping for air.
Everything is sucked towards the twister,
dust, leaves, memories, tumbleweed away.

I recognize you across the field.
You glow against the spinning dark,
one hand cups a match with no flame,
yet I see your shadowed eyes.

       I would race like a cloud to gather you safely in
but it's already too late.
You're way beyond the shadow.
The roar is deafening. You turn
and climb easily among the others.

The rugs are up

geography blown apart.
No familiar ponds and islands,
no fringing reeds.

Naked floorboards disclose
cracks and knot-holes,
a catalogue of minor loss:
   rusty needle
   peanut
   earring
   trail of fluff and thread
and more still underneath.

Here is the secret side of furniture,
unadorned surfaces meant to face the wall,
unpolished wood behind cabinets,
dust-drifted artefacts down on the floor.

Where are the lotus-filled pools,
the nearly-birds on angular branches
pretending not to be
representational?

Rolled up they can't reflect the sky
but reveal the curving undersides
of lilies, leaves and waterfowl,
the working underbelly of peace
in the gardens of paradise.

event horizon

(after the Antony Gormley installation around Waterloo Bridge in 2007)

they stand on the skyline
on flat-topped buildings
(as if) the remnants
of an army just landed
down-tilted heads observe

the river – gatekeeper
the bridge – familiar
the roundabout – transitional
the built environment – imposed
the people – in their own image

hurry north and south
eyes rise to recognize
figures appear disappear
behind the constructs
chimney stacks   lift-housings   steam vents

re-emerge somehow
changed re
-condite -formed -distanced
(dis)passionate regard
settling on the day's resolve

Confession

Fairytale hair drifts round
porcelain skin, gentle cheeks,
plump flesh taut to the bone,
eyes downcast in modesty.
A gown of sky-blue pink, frilled
with the innocence of childhood.
Softly touch the eyes, the lips.

Or – pick a scalpel from the tray,
search the flawless complexion
for an entry point to puncture.
Jab a needle where there are no pores
and hear the hiss of escaping air.
Go deeper, probe, insert cold steel,
peel back to the subcutaneous void.

Place your eye to the inner optic
to view the implosion of matter,
the endless destruction of stars,
extermination, corruption, emanating
from the real face underneath;
the reeking leather darkness,
the toxic blood, the desolation.

Space is warped by my presence

You put me here with a cup and an inkwell,
told me to drink in the stillness.

I misremember why I'm here.
In the emptiness you left, windows keep out the light,

which never changes, falls from the wrong sources,
never moves across the floor.

It doesn't ease the dark or disperse the black granules,
even above the fog the obdurate headstones push through.

However softly they move, I can't hear you
behind the gnashing of their bones.

We never speak except at night. I wait for my voice,
poison in your ear.   The hiss.

Oversight

I don't reflect anywhere
so I can't check my mouth,
but although the stretch hurts,
I know it generally smiles
in a passable way. I am likeable.

For which reason I wear denim, not silk
and although you wouldn't know it,
my clothes are carefully designed
to look friendly and acceptable without
giving up on superiority.

I can see your eyes flicker over me
checking the exact template, blueprint.
I assess which of you will fit the bill.
My range is further, I have wider eyes,
and more than these two you can see.

Tomorrow you will regret this oversight.
I will reveal my origins, my provenance.
When I remove these ordinary garments
you will see my scales, my iridescence.
Hypnotised by my beauty, you will follow.

Fulcrum

I disbelieve your smile, translate
your outstretched palm as itching to slap me,
muscles twitching for an alternative fist.

Or is it my internal putrefaction
that colours perception, yours and mine?
You sense my position imposing on the air,
tearing angular holes like a cartoon cat.

It's a dietary issue, I trigger anaphylactic shock
in you, choke you till you explode,
shooting dum-dum bullets into my brain.
Hit, I spin past the possibilities of every direction.

I will not settle my compass point.
The needle wobbles on its pivot, useless
if it stops seeking true north

White Night

(after Robert Frost)

A thing so small could make the terror swell,
a tiny glimpse into the broken dark.
Such random specks of insignificance
show leaks of too much white through midnight's wall,
whose base is carpeted with dry dead wings.
A chilling note of doubt cracks sleep apart,
pattern of darkness pushes back the pall
of blank malevolence in place of God,

freezes the moment as a paper kite
believes it rules the air before the fall;
fell utterance around the witches' pot
configures future hope into its thrall.
No vestige left of light nor level breath,
pale intricate designs disguise the path.

In the Mansions of the Dead

Every morning the soul rushes to the window
fading into the last wisp of dream.
It thuds against the strictures singed in light,
nudges the body, treacle-slow
in the shower, clad in steam,
rubbing out the residue of night.

The soul bruises against walls,
chafes and scratches every surface.
Imprisoned claustrophobe
trapped in the body's thrall
as it turns through space
on an unbalanced globe.

Every morning the window vanishes
into fumes, cacophony, congestion.
The answer diminishes,
if there was ever a question.

mother of pearl

small sun flares
disappears
light years away
gritting space
with dust invisible
to earth eyes surfing
the middle distance
without aim or interest
till migrant particles
irritate the humours
stimulate protection
oystering a pearl
not lucid but reflective
of the infinite mother
spiralling about us

Madonna Suffused With Glory

Sleeping *putti* piled like kittens sinking into each other
under the watchful gaze of a very confused virgin.
What could you believe of someone who insists
her son chats with cherubim, or will do in his future and ours
and might even raise the dead and certainly see many
fall in his name, so it's just as well he can,
or so she claims.

But see how she holds the fragile bud
between her thumb and index finger – not tightly at all.
It hovers there in possibility, like everything she says.
Does she think she is the mother of God, or does He
brand her with gurgled blessings from the manger?
Epiphanies are still born from nipple and lip, deification.
Glory fades with vesper.
How will you face the dark?

Tubby Beek

The long-nosed Tubby Beek
and his attendant transparency touch down
where what transparency can achieve
without the interference of light,
and what light itself can do
at the very end of the afternoon,
unveils thresholds
at the moment when dust occludes
the outer surface of the eyeball
and spherical aberration transforms
everything on the cusp to constellations
and dusk bows to the predominance of light
continuing forever
on its infinite journey through the parallels,
then Tubby Beek, O remember –
in whatever universe you vibrate,
your jewelled note is always more beautiful
than its setting.

Not dead but gone to sleep

The Reaper has already passed,
yet his scythe has forgotten
where and why
the grass here is so lush.
Vetches weave through comfrey and groundsel,
clustered grasses curve over gravestones,
thatch above roosting birds,
keep their distance
from the shadowed mausoleums.

The multitude of stems are massed
around stones where long-written
lines still try
to deny the sudden hush
fallen on torn lives. They keep their counsel
banal or prettified: *gone to sleep alone,*
where to find the words
asleep in Jesus' hands
gives no comfort or reason.

Not gone to sleep, but dead.

Sailing past the cemetery

Ghosts atop cypressed walls watch the ground-row
towers and domes grow delicate fretworked cranes
gliding cut stones into the landscape, swinging freight.
The waterbright sky crisscrossed by passing trails,
skyfilled lagoon by chevron wakes and dying waves;
everything requisite engraves the air with mystery.

History slides past vessels laden with sentient cargo
transported from pillar to portico to palazzo in a daze
of selfie sticks, haze of ill-aimed lenses clocks the view.
How the light slews around them! How the memories!
Ersatz colours, instant framed facsimiles, blanched
remnants of drenched intensity periscoped back home.

Brims tipped and shadows sought to fool the sun.
Souls flare away from the Island of the Dead.

Stone Tank

It brimmed with mystery in its corner of the garden,
so near invisible in deepest shadow.
Foliage dense with reflections blotted sky
from the surface it patted so delicately,
tickling the thousand-legged critters
splayed on the caul of water.
Crows karked at sun-cracks in the shade,
dropped to the edge to drink with beady confidence.
For us it was taboo, even to trail hands
in siesta heat, for we would surely suck the wetness
from our fingers, lick its clammy freight of cells,
the sliding horrors forever creeping down our guts.
The whoop of brainfever birds climbed higher and higher
into marigold air, started over, clamoured up the sky.

PART II

The Fall of Light

Rapid Eye Movement

Walk up the hill past the stone houses
where pavement dwellers smile,
hairpin bend towards the old palace
my mother visited,
heavy with a too-cosy baby,
the many staircases
meant to shake it out of comfort
into the opulence of life –
                                        but I digress –

a hundred yards after the palace
turn into a quiet road cross-hatched
with shade and driveways
leading to cliff-top houses,
above them translucent wings
sweep an unreachable dome.

Look over the ant-hill city and back,
to find its upper levels swaying close,
termites become strolling princes,
huts flowered into terraced Xanadus
still climbing up towards the sky,
away from exhaust fumes and flames
of oil refineries, the reek of the dye pits,
the pungency of fish-drying poles.

Everything rises to heaven, lingers
under the unbreachable dome.

Blind Light

I am light as happiness,
surrounded by light,
enough to float away untethered.
Light upgrades the outlook.
The light-filled lagoon strikes blindly,
ignorant of where it strikes or if it wounds.
Seas lighten into morning, outlook stormy.
Lightning flicks and jags into water,
shelters its light beneath a thin cagoule
the colour of change.

The colour of change
shelters its light beneath a thin cagoule.
Lightning flicks and jags into water,
seas lighten into morning, outlook stormy.
Ignorant of where it strikes or if it wounds
the light-filled lagoon strikes blindly.
Light upgrades the outlook,
enough to float away untethered,
surrounded by light,
I am light as happiness.

Sisyphus at the birth of a tower crane

Little cranes toss metal and concrete
into a growing tower scaffolding
itself up and up, sliding up and down,
bearing down and down,
burying support into quiescent ground.

The tip moves further away
from its small progenitors, willing
this next generation skyward.
Rising confidently from its own
limits, it edges into infinity.

The finished tower pirouettes,
carrying the built environment
heavenwards, its own constellations
mapped red against the night,
warning of the violation of the sky.

The target vaults over the framework,
looking down at the tallest crane.

The Secret Life of Cranes

The cranes are humping tonight.
They've turned on the red lights,
lit candles in the high cabins
quivering among the stars.

Cries of passion arch
over distant rooftops,
splash down in moonlight
between riverboats and waterfowl.

Girders tremble, chains bang,
locked elevators strain upwards,
break free and mount
the scaffolding to watch

what happens in the sky
while they work the erections
up and down from hell to heaven
and back to bump the earth,

grinding mechanical slump,
turned off, powered down,
inanimate starveling,
access denied.

nomad

unwinding a road
towards its vanishing point
nomad   no name
moving forward step by step
through slow vineyards
old orchards   magnetic skies
spooled horizons unwinding

nomad of the nacreous eyes
resting where goats balance
spilling sweet water into rock pools
gazelles spring their thirst
down molten cliffs
stop on the edge
lower their necks
fold their legs
to enter their reflections
to drink small flames
quenched

Light is the guiding light

Amazed by the luggage of travellers
I no longer have strength for burdens.
Home is floating away
from memory, light diminishes.
I wait for transport to carry me
over invisible landscape
but no one can see me standing
eclipsed by my own thrown shadow
my back to the hope of sun.

morning slide

just before sun-up
everything disguised
in night mercury
flows towards day
slips through the sash
into eddies and thermals
stirs and riffs off the canopy
shakes out the shift-changers
        circadian rhythms
swapped on day's edge
wings clatter and hum
weavers throw silk
to the light shimmying
through permeable walls
engines sputter and cough
dark cracks open
round visible birds
        suddenly shelterless

Random Access Memory

In the stippled sky landing lights of planes circle the city waiting for a hole in the storm. They spin the white strands, turn them faster and faster, whip the air like candyfloss into a maelstrom that starts to suck up the metropolis, detaching churches and offices, tower cranes and semis, council blocks, cinemas and homeless shelters, till there is nothing left but an emptiness undulating into the distance. A scattering of people stare into the space above them. Everything is silent. Even the planes are gone.

Where do I look for refuge?
An hour ago was rich in comforts,
warmth, friends, future.
All gone into the vortex.
Where are the birds, the foxes?
Where the cattle, the fodder, the beacons?
Have the tormentors survived?
Is my lover in this desolation?

Tundra plants cluster together to resist the cold. The snow protects them. Growing seasons are brief, so most plants reproduce by budding and division rather than sexually.

my thighs redden
with the venom
of polar winds
seeking crudely
under my skirt

the place of our first kiss
frozen in memory

the buried station
a sanctuary
one lonely light
beneath the ice

Emperor Penguin

I balance the future on my instep,
warm it under my blubber.

Shuffling slowly, I try to keep it
from falling and freezing.

I move with my thousand-bodied tribe
rotating minutely to and from the hub

of safety, trusting the darkness.
Antarctic winter pivots around me.

I accept the settlement of ice
over the hunger of my body.

I do not consider the return of light,
my mate, or food. The future

will crack open at my feet.
I will return to the ocean.

Ex Libris

Before the sun lowers itself enough,
before its cast shadows leave my page,
before it's too dark to read,
a tiny white bug runs across the print,
turns under page 23 and disappears.

I don't close the book for a while,
stare at the pale rectangle
in front of my eyes, fading
till I shut and lay it down,
turn on lights, draw curtains.

Maybe I'll have time in the morning,
maybe I'll finish a chapter with coffee.
Maybe I won't find a smear –
its tiny white bookmark.

Scumble

(after Gerard Manley Hopkins)

Thank God for fluff-tumbled corners,
    cobwebbed shadows beneath undusted windows,
        grainy patches of light on scuffed floorboards,
            an archive of colours under peeling paint.
Delight in the decrepit: warped timbers, skewed view,
    angles below tables fringed with lamplight.
Breathe in the senseless spaces of stairwells,
        Run fingers over the sheen of pointless carving.

Praise the lovely uselessness of ridge tiles,
    kitchens with unflush cupboards standing proud
        or withdrawn, their unreachable crannies.
Follow the polyphony of birdsong deep
    into green tunnels, unpulled weeds, wildflowers.
Fade into rampant ivy, sink into unkempt grass
        stare at unbiddable clouds, unruly rain.
            Sublime.

early hours

leaves are not opaque
this summer dawn
letting the light slide
fresh from rooftops
into the canopy and down
from branch to bush
not shadowing but
themselves turned into
green transparencies
projecting every running
overlap and overleap
the start of viridescent birds
rustling without a word
everything swells and sings

not spiders enough to hang
so much silk from plant to plant
connect leaf-edge to leaf-edge
stem to stamen to petal
no way through
such fine filaments visible
only when light glides
along the threads or
floats through early air
neither to settle nor to fly
with swallows in the insect sky
yet to carry the tiny caterpillar
spinning and casting to and from
the swell of apples not yet ripe.

Bluebell Woods

Even in well-trodden London
there are intervals of woodland,
where the bee-drone of traffic
is snuffed out by the sough of leaves.
Cathedral shafts of moted sun
cut through the canopy,
glitter with insect wings,
particles circling in light.

Busy Londoner that you are,
you hurry forward into a blur
of reticulated blue and green.
Underfoot the swell
to the next rise and dip
spills you onward into an ocean
spindrifted with flecks of light,
until your time is up, you must turn back,

but find the path behind you
transformed, translucent.
Every leaf and petal, blade of grass,
singing with knowledge
of the light they live and die in
and the rooted trees
sink into the radiance, overcome
by the embrace of light.

The Sixth Day

Day one, number one, essential –
before everything there was Light.
But the sixth day was astounding.
After countless try-outs,
rejects and selections,
those eyes opened golden and deep,
a pelt of gold-barred shadow
muscled exquisitely over feline frame,
silent on great pads of velvet and claw.
O Tiger, most beautiful of creation,
just as lamb, slug, mealy bug and man,
all that lives and moves,
crammed onto this trembling earth.
Even the stars paled.

Trashcan Tumbler

In the plush purple cloak I wear at midnight
I go on forays with my favourite cat,
who is so fond of Emmental cheese
that we always end up by the dustbins

of the Swiss café quarter.
Graceful tumbler of the trashcans,
he vaults from stack to stack of stinking rubbish
with a determination I find consoling.

Such serendipity is in the bins!
He tosses aside plastic and paper
to vanish among rinds and wrappers
sent from the mountains of a pristine State.

He emerges, delicately shaking his paws.
Persuaded by the confabulation
of his onomatopoeic comments,
I follow the flare of his tail up the alley.

Squirrelling Away

They bombard me with grapes, exploding shells
and seeds, a constant barrage through branches
they seem to choose purely for ambush.
Wilful poses, from Beatrix to Disney,
eyes downcast only because I am below,
for they have no modesty in their enjoyment
of the profligate summer's end.

Ignorant that these plump moments
will wither into twigs against a lowering sky
and they will have recourse to winter berries
old wives believe are plentiful because *the coming
months will be uncommon bleak and cold*,
they leap from tree to bush to tree,
winking at pigeons clumsily drowning
in elder, too full of juice to care
that earth tilts further from the sun.

Witch Hazel

Dark-glisten gold
detonates the branches,
hazes the air around them,
spindling from the stem
to air still winter-cold.

Petals high-step, stretch
and curl, drenched
in spring's imminence,
tippled and sucked,
drunk on the essence
of witchery, shoot
across their own heart,
blood-clotted centre,
heavy with light.

Kerria

Brave new buds shrug
out of sticky twigs,
shake out frills,
flirt their petticoats,
spread their petals
wide to the sun,
shimmy velvet flesh
soft in the breeze.

In the tall blue sky
changing clouds pile
upon themselves,
dark with desire
to touch the blossom,
violate its bloom.

listen for the river in a goldfish bowl

you come around again
loop the tiny castle
nose the chest of jewels
inspect the tinted gravel
fronds of plastic seaweed

in your search for crumbs
do you spindrift through
dreams of golden rivers
swirling through rainforest
the slither roar and tumble
of deep green-marbled water

as you circle your space
what do you see beside you
in the curving glass

Nightshade

Sea licks along a shore
sand shifted long ago.
Pebbles coerce the earth
where salt weeds perch
round frail blooms and frills
of thick-sinewed seakale.
Upright stems gibbet
the horizon like warriors' ghosts.

Night shades the beach. Purple
umbels hang against cloud,
suck toxins from primordial depths
pumped into clustered berries.
Thrusting yellow tongues
taste blood in the waves.

Tide

Seas are parting but only to receive the dead, bodies
falling over themselves to get to something better,
the future impetus behind the past in tatters.
Boom and crash and darkness in the air
impel them onwards to a tumbling shore.

Gummy-eyed sleep ebbs from bodies
seizing the avid headlines round the capsize
of the hour and the papers crumple and scatter lies
inside thin jackets stuffed against shortening days,
sun slides back to warmer latitudes, earth turns away.

Ink squeezes bubbles from the heart and bodies
bleed in every colour, every ocean, every way.
Dark waves roil up, blotting out the sky,
break over borders, blur the lines, divide.
Not peace nor war can quell the rising tide.

The Wretchedness of Crows

At night I hear the wretchedness of crows,
in the day their voices of distress.
There's danger in the ocean, this they know
and rasp a warning not to go across.
A jagging fracture pulls the sea apart,
broken waters gather dark and rise.
Crows fathom both the issue and the start.
From the fissure pours a mortal tide.
The gathered force increases from behind,
and juggernauts a path through sea and air.
Desperation grows and flees the land
and sets itself adrift and drowns at war.
The crows, unheeded, mourn these wasted lives
and mark the footprints leading to the waves.

Roofbeams

Anyway, they bought the shell,
hung the bricks with colourful throws
and scores of lamps that lent a glow
of *gemütlichkeit* to the lack of substance
but they noticed that the walls were shrinking
away from the roof, which floated
on in spite of the lack of communication.
At night light spilled from the eves,
quite stunning from the outside,
even more so when the roof stretched
and rays shot out between the tiles
and although they enjoyed sleeping
under syncopated stars and moon phases,
they were relieved it was a dry summer.

When the cold came they got a quote
for pulling things together, gulped
at the figures and lit more lamps
against the shortening days,
not realising that their private life
seeped onto the pavement through the gaps,
till the watchers in the street intruded
on their questionable idyll.

The question answered: monetise it,
vlog it to the titillated, stimulate high interest
to raise the roof and reinforce the walls.
Success was suffocating in its use of space.

They rented out their porous home
and moved to Minnesota to avoid the storms.

Get over yourself

Kick over the microscope,
stop staring at your pretty coloured fractals.
In a world of blinding contrast
who hides in the calibrations, who moves
over the tone chart, however slowly?

Give thought to the progress of others,
how to avoid the pratfalls, yours and theirs.
If you move your feet over the earth
they'll get you from somewhere
to somewhere else, however slowly.

Consider this kneeling woman
who watches over two generations,
trying to reverse the peril.
She gathers up nothing but memories
and advances, however slowly.

Stretch

This stretch of wall has seen a lot
but stops her from seeing much
more than its mucky bricks.
In the alley they brace and heave
next to the overflowing trash.
Cats are more fastidious, seldom
grooming on the lids and not,
certainly not, watching the show.
On hot nights windows stay closed,
the stench of piss too ripe
to savour any cooling breeze.
Mostly she sits and stares
at the compromised grouting,
loses herself in the micro-life
struggling for light and water,
the delicate leaves and lichens
somehow surviving, thrusting
perpendicular to perpendicular,
over tiny patches of stars
on the fired earth cosmos.
Starved for the sight of sky
she wills herself Lilliputian
to lose herself in the forests,
crystal grottos, unfamiliar blooms,
strains with them upwards.
       She hears the door behind her
       bang, the creak and the zip.

Dissolve

It is a given that rain
will dissolve everything
you hold dear today.
Tomorrow you won't –

When the sun shines
in spite of the difficulties,
remove the coverings,
polish the roses,
walk into the blown mirror.

You could be losing
if you allow the clouds.
Consider how things look
in the dark. Do you see,
do you see?
You could so easily flip
the switch until morning.

Accept that in light
is the right place to rest
and that's going
to be harder
and harder.

Seed the clouds,
fall as rain,
dissolve.

Camera Obscura

when I was small I never knew
I would grow this big

I'm in the way of the light
the old stories are twisted
into invisibility

I need the curve of wood under the arches of my feet
and the true names
that hold the parameters steady

if I lose concentration
the innocence of bird and brute will alter
the cheerful crackling on the hearth

as the trees close in
small creatures crawl out of the floorboards
drop from the branches

stream away among the trunks
the roots the darkness
I am the darkest thing in here

whatever is visible
obscures everything else
the coloratura chimney screams

don't be fooled by the silence
the beast is out there
I can see the gleam of its eyes

reflected in this small bottle
when I hold it away from the flames
if I see more I'm in trouble

tonight I sat down at the edge
of the clearing
pulled the long grass around me

when they burned it down
the trees facing me were charred and twisted
their far sides still green and lush

If I don't want to see
I should open my eyes

Life in the camp

I wasn't there but
my surviving family
told me what happened

And so I pray

Peril paints the horizon and thuds
into the ground while I butter my toast.
My soulmates slide to the edge of life.
I have no shield to hold over the beloved.
No echo returns from the future.

Then the sun turns a dirty London corner
and conjures a luminous cityscape
from cracks in the concrete.
Neglected crannies fill with incandescent dust.
Radiance flickers over unsettled faces.

So I pray to give the dead the love they deserved,
to inhabit, like a hoverfly, my own speck of heaven,
for my cat to hurry slowly towards me,
my man to touch me for no reason,
for the ocean, for the air, for the restoration of love.

PART III

Worry Beads

the letter was shredded before it was written

the brain parted company with the hand
the hand with the fingers
the dropped pen
the wrong keys

punched

I am the key he told her years before
inserting himself easily
into the lock

like he had solved the riddle
in the fairy tale
eschewing   the deadlocks
                   gold curlicues
                   diamond studs
himself the perfect answer
the solution to her

                    looking back she bridled
bumped off the maiden
voyage on the slipway

            her hotel room has a digital key
            plastic anonymous ingress
            everyone faceless at the door
                    both sides know

Fuck you she mouths   *my call now*

portrait with badly-drawn birds

she tries to avoid them
    but the ravens are always with her
beady-eyed in the looking glass
       she turns her back on the evidence
       hangs the mirrors high
but in them life continues in spite

after the flood she squelches through silt
drags the boat out onto the lake   pulls at the oars
     ravens settle the prow   watching

somewhere he will be searching too
with customary certainty   always in the wrong direction
   not knowing the little cadaver flickering
beside her leaking still into the submerged landscape

she wants to give up the effort of reflection
now she can see herself
            sink   through glass-smooth surface
   but the head-tilt of the birds reveals the point of her
descent   refracts upwards from a mirror's crack
      through ghosts misting the lower air
             the ravens take flight

The Genuine Article

Stop running
your monkey toes along the edge.
You need to trim your nails and polish
inside this frame you chose.
Before you arrived
you barely knew yourself
outside the glossy pages,
expensive ink oozing
sweetly-fragranced promises,
aspirational articles
defining   the
indefinite.
An
indefinite
defining   the
aspirational articles,
sweetly-fragranced promises,
expensive ink oozing
outside the glossy pages.
You barely knew yourself
before you arrived
inside this frame you chose.
You need to trim your nails and polish
your monkey toes along the edge.
Stop running.

wonderland

I don't often notice the dirt
flaking ivory
paint on metal
but it hides a hole
into the system
gurgling pipework
underground mould

I reach in with my index
feel mushroom velvet
fingernail a paring out into the room

       Alice taught me well so I eat it

                shoot through wonderland

          sunlight dissipates the dankness   the sewers blossom
          with jasmine   burgeoning crystals   microscopic buds
          burst into bloom   everything slants away

I ride fresh light through dilations and distances where nothing reflects
    but cosmic dust

Consider the Mantis

('I shall praise your mandibles first', from: 'I was a Gentleman Botanist', The Confessions, Christopher DeWeese)

I shall praise your mandibles first
that moved so lustfully, nibbled my edges,
softened them for your lips to suck out independent thought.

I shall praise your mandibles
but first I shall remove my shoes, although
I'm not sure why – maybe to give independent movement to my toes.

I shall praise your
mandibles first, eyelids next, lips third, as a corner lifts
in what might be a sneer to unnerve; bedroom eyes droop.

I shall praise…
your mandibles first came to mind as I watched your Adam's Apple;
my incisors hummed – I can't think why this should be.

I shall
not praise you, or your mandibles –
you do an excellent job yourself –
I'm too busy looking for independence.

I
do not praise your mandibles
or feed your impulse to sneer, droop,
your eyelids I mean – or do I?

Conjurer

My Father wrote to us in the voices of two crows,
who watched him with cocked heads and thoughtful eyes.
Jimmy and Priscilla on the verandah rail
squawked their comments on pale blue onionskins
that flew across the great green waters
to the damp grey island of our exile.
We huddled around the warmth that flooded out
as we tore open the flimsy paper
and streams of light conjured up
bougainvillea, flame of the forest,
frangipani and heavy rose.
The hot afternoon vibrated,
polychromatic, polyphonic, aromatic.
When we finished reading the glow faded,
dismal day returned and we froze,
two little match girls in the cold.

Melancholy

(with apologies to Keats)

Don't even think of it, the dark river.
Flush the tablets, turn off the gas,
tip the garden poisons in the compost.

Shiver in delight at the owl's cry,
the miserable rain – you're a part of it,
hard-wired to melancholy.

When your lover bites your head off,
peppers you with reproaches,
she won't scoff you like a mantis.

Instead, you'll have great make-up sex,
burst the grape, taste the salt,
reflect in her mirror, a cloudy trophy.

Muscle

Her muscles try to decompress her heart
constrained so cruelly within his grasp.
To emphasise his needs he makes a fist
and bangs it on the table once, then hits
her chest. Her heart convulses in his hand,
it hurts, *it hurts*, his fingers crush the sound
thump-*thud,* beat-*pound* the breath out of distress.
Her rib-cage crumbles over emptiness.

fingernails can't take the strain

close your eyes only to blink
                    you need to clock your route
          not because you want to mark the way back

this is a red-eye ride   you may not know
      where you're going
                        that ambiguity ahead of you   slo-mo
    opening onto something   beautiful   or suffocating
take your pick
                        of which eye to use
            its perspective   colour   depth
edit your astigmatic view   tilt your head to see
          what stretches   what curves

        slide   on the saddle
    this jolting can't be good for the spine
take care
          not to grip your fingertips into your mount
          you might draw blood

      whatever that was that was   that   falling
behind messily   don't look back
              tense your thighs to stay forward   never be gentle
          with yourself
          you may be water on stone

Wonder Woman discovers her gills

unfluffy princess in starry shorts
          not flying but leaping up on currents of air
reading the thermals
lariat glowing at her hip
strong and fearless

seven years burned beneath my own black hair
          I leapt under water to fly
sputtered up after my distance expired
                              fled to the edge of safety
believing hostile air would drown me

                    until I surfaced too far
not drowning but floating
half relinquished
by the glassy green
I rolled up to glaring blue

and back to the supporting deep
          soared down into currents of power
reading the thermals
until breath ran out
through new discovered gills

In the end

                all his maps, blueprints and slide rules
couldn't stop me from flying south.

I looked down onto waterways polishing continents,
chose a river for its tributaries, the lustre of its flows to the sea,
dived through the surface, believing I could breathe
better underwater.

Full moon lengthened the shadows.
I constructed paper boats
from books discarded on the riverbank,
filled them with red palm oil, lit them,
followed the tiny lights
along the forest wall where it edged the water.

Towards the estuary the shoreline broke into flame,
reached across the wavelets to set them on fire too.
Titanic blacksmiths crashed hammers into iron cliffs,
cities rose from the forges, scaffolds encrusted with sparks.

                *

When I left the city I left the city but it followed
me, bereft, till I turned and returned, walking back
over the bloodied landscape.

Maybe I don't need water to cover my head.
My city stands in the ocean, reflecting.

Cheer up love, it might never happen

Except you are a chrysanthemum leering
over the wall I walk beside, so it has.

Here is an over-pollarded tree suffocating
in plastic, punching its outline for air.
Here is a branch, rigid, dead,
broken. How do I not weep at the sight
of this small body strewn in the path
before the storm which will break
so many others?
                        Only a branch, my love,
only a branch in the brain's topography.

Promises are powerless, it may *not* be ok.
I can't wait for the next morning glory
to blow my mind clear of dread, so hold me
up to the light, check my transparency
against the original blueprint.

Old Vines

Smashed panes let in the weather but
it watered your tattered garments, your roots.
Unfamiliar lichens staunched your wounds,
microscopic life cracked into your brickwork,
forced it to let go, allow the incomers
to festoon you in gold and green
and the last of the vine burst out
of hiding, tendrils supplicating.
You accepted the offerings:
wild geraniums, agrimony, mallow,
garlands of daisies.
Now your crumbling spaces
are squatted and daubed with colour.
You lean against the old wall, listen
to the gossip and flaunt your new finery
at the ancient trees across the valley.

No Direction

On the plane back to Shanghai from Jingdezhen there is so much porcelain
carried on by the passengers, that the lavatory is requisitioned to store it.

A runaway train was deliberately derailed in Western Australia, after 50
minutes of travelling at 70 mph with no one on board.

If the accusations are groundless, dementia may have set in.

We carry such a weight of errors. How should we face the future?

Trickle-Down Effect

Old worlds are smashed by satirists and slaves
trying to fudge the mould, distort the glass;
a pain to riders high on fortune's surf,
who thought their luck would carry them to shore.
But water is fragmentary, can break
apart, convert the journey, maelstrom life.
Washed up they pound the sidewalks and the bars
in slippers someone else wore down-at-heel,
rattle a dented cup for crumbs and coins,
assimilate the spittle on fate's chin
to demonstrate how wealth can dribble down.

Libertine

What used to be called a gentleman —
is opposed — to technical — professional — or special training.
It will be best to dispose first of — daily — conversation
among all who have not been taught to avoid it —
a matter of care and study rather than — right instinct —
a — vulgar — slovenly — figure — has — risen — imperfectly drawn —
the — fellow drank — brandy intended for those
who — wish to avoid — similar questionable uses —

Most of those now — have no subordinate —
a defence — neither plausible nor satisfactory —
the unquestioned — second — and fourth types are faulty
and represent neglect — gentlemen, their political title —
is — beyond dispute — unlike last year —
dying children suddenly appear

(redacted from pp 334/5 Fowler's Modern English Usage, second edition)

Worry Beads

First, carefully extract the livid jelly.
At this stage the lobes must remain intact.
Coax them out with the sensitive tips of your fingers.
To combat the effect on your hands, sprinkle liberally with salt.

Choose the ones that look most surprised,
any already wilting should be discarded.
This is quite slow, frustrating work
but the results are well worth the effort.

Lay the lobes gently in a well-oiled mortar.
It is advisable to treat the pestle as well.
Add two ghost chillies, or one Trinidad Scorpion chilli
(wear protective gloves for this).

Grind, firmly at first, gradually decreasing the pressure
until you feel no further resistance.
When the mixture attains the consistency of bread dough,
the chilli fragments well distributed

but not too uniform in size (texture is everything here),
turn onto a ceramic chopping board. Still wearing the gloves,
divide and roll into palm-sized nuggets
and wrap these copiously, but not too tightly, in clingfilm.

Choose two nuggets, place one in each pocket
(*caution:* any small change could cause damage), freeze the rest.
The loose wrapping allows you to prod and mould them at will,
Clingfilm protects your clothes from stains.

When a package begins to disintegrate,
take another from the freezer.
Defrost completely at room temperature
before attempting to replace the redundant ball.

Even the tea leaves give nothing away

The rain that drowned the earthworms
passed without comment.
The rain that drowned the baby
caused questions in the house.

I have to sit here every day
since they brought me home.
They tell me it is dangerous
to bathe, or to throw myself in.

I watch the same man pass by at noon,
hear the pebbles crunch with each step
he takes above last night's rain
draining back into the inlet.

The cup is empty and I am thirsty.
Even the tea-leaves give nothing away.
His hands are busy in his pockets
with worry beads of rain.

Wherever I look he is moving away.
I try to tether him to earth
but the guy-ropes snap
and he leaves me, taking the keys.

I'm still watching the hot rain pour
off the eaves,
a curtained doorway,
open.

Thaumaturgy

That day on the asteroid would be the last day
I spent this way, searching for discarded hexes,
licks and spells, drained beyond hunger.

Among them I noticed one   still slightly glowing,
showing signs of power but not smouldering.
Shouldering my sack I gathered it carefully,
fearful that it might burn me to the bone.

It shone in my hand, cautiously warm.
A sentient charm then. I could feel its core
suspire, sending out echoes,
flows of potential, seeking the sense
of its existence.   So before it could effloresce,
I forced it into my index thimble, loosened
my fleece and stamped off the occult glister
and dust, ignoring their mumbles
as they tumbled through the microcosm,
rune-chrism smoking around them.   I thrust
off, blasted towards the pump house lights,
brighter than the little moon it stood upon.
I won my prize, delivered my thimbleful of magic,
to the dozing front desk indwellers, to earn
my churning bag of fortune.   So now I live
on my own sliver of moon, with commands
on my hands, barely lifting my little fingers.

Yet… I linger at the window facing the trash-towers,
watch showers of meteors over the winking landfill,
will them to crash down, blow it to smithereens,
wither the necromancy, and release the last thaumaturge
to surge through the flak and conjure the first day.

Consequential waves unsettle the galaxy

how did I get here

I didn't choose this Little Prince miniplanet.
I don't know its name, it probably doesn't have one,
maybe I'll dub it something myself.

who names the stars   can a planet be tamed

Till I find my space legs I've jammed myself between
a rock and a tree, sure I'll fall off if I move.

I am held between smooth marble
*   roughbarked tree*
it whispers to my ear against the trunk
telling of its seven ages of creation
balance and unbalance

The day rushes past into a brief night behind it,
penumbra hovers under an infinite starcloth.

I work with the 8th age of the asteroid
the thinning trees let in more light
I give love and respect to the shy water god
clear her pools
prime her concomitant fountains

Around this one is a scattering of other small planets
spinning in a haze of icecream colours,
yet I'm not dizzy

I trail my hands in the coolth and look towards
Pistachio Vanilla Tuttifrutti   nicknamed by me
in banal reference to how they colour my nights
fill my tumbling days with delight

until I see the space between isn't empty,
is solid roiling texture, a moaning background,
a dull red danger, a giant planet
for which we tiny, overlooked moons
are of no importance, to be swatted away like pests.

insignificant to the universe
why am I so hugely here

I recognize the righteous lumbering of growth.
Cracks in the surface lengthen, split, spit,
slalom recklessly from weakness to weakness.

I have no power

Red Giant with exhausted core, unstable,
threatening this corner of space; just this corner   for now.
Invasive flame dendrites from the monster

the icecream moonlets melt
In this corner of space, just here, just now,
there will be damage

I call my little planet   *Beloved*

PART IV

Out of Kilter

Picture Gallery

Here's the floor plan, a simplified map
leading to the paintings via squares,
straight lines, small print, frames of reference.
Follow and find, walk through the arch
into a gathering of favourites, a collection
of remembered shapes and colours
lifting from the walls, *through* the walls,
erasing the ceiling, pushing back the sky.

Space expands, horizons recede,
only breath shortens. Cartography:
here be dragons, madonnas and mythologies,
lamplit interiors, physiognomies, seascapes.
Two-dimensional contours curve the earth,
star-chart our visions up and beyond.

Icicles in the Frame

It's hard to remember before the ash cloud.
Then, whenever he left home, he would check
and recheck the gas, the electricity, the keys.

Now he dosses on a bench opposite the Museum,
wakes each day to endless winter, breaks
through the night's fall of snow, drags himself
upright, thumping the sleeves of his frozen overcoat.

He skids his way carefully up the steps to the portico,
hands deep in stiff pockets, reassured
but not warmed by their contents.

In front of the paintings he forgets the cold
scraping his bones, claiming his flesh.
These icicle-framed scenes are increasingly chilly
under their clinking glaze.

He stands in a puddle of slush drizzling from his hem.
Move along sir, you'll trigger the alarms. But they both know
they have no more power. His footsteps glitter the marble.

sixty percent   diminishing

I used to boil it first   bottled in the fridge
but now there's no fridge
nor even dirty water to purify

when the dam broke   that was it for power
but   everything behind it
    where did it go

the river bed is deep with dust
and families working the erratic holes
I must go out to collect   something

unsound rock and broken skeletons
don't make much progress
who can knit the bones…

god   for the comfort of chimneys
where there's smoke there's hope
but no flume spills from ravine to sky

little movement anywhere to the high horizon
only faded plastic bunting signals persistently
outside the cliff-cut caves

is it still dark outside
what shall I do when the sun comes up
maybe   if I exit backwards   I can fly

Waste, a Growing Problem

Report from Peripatetic Inspector to Great Inventor of Waste Particle Transmogrification

<u>Example 1</u>

On this planet – Earth – periods designated Break or Recreation
are not for breaking down the old and turning it into something new.
It is when Earthlings (Humans) mix liquid chemicals to pour into their faces,
or tear open paper and plastic containers, push their fingers through,
to grab and carry the contents as fast as possible into the same place.

This is called drinking and eating and is one of the main causes of waste.

> <u>First</u>: because most of what goes into the face (drink and food)
> is surplus to requirement and thrown away *[Appendix 15, Overload]*.

> <u>Second</u>: waste exits the body with – mostly – a changed appearance,
> considered unviewable, unspeakable, and certainly it smells bad.
> The common name for this is shit, which must be removed at once.

> *[<u>Note</u>: for other words – synonyms – for shit, see Appendix 39]*.

Humans have been inventive about shit removal, but it is a waste of time
[Appendix 52, Leisure] as it merely pushes the problem further down the line.
Shit is washed through a country-wide grid of water-flushed pipes called sewers,
to be either farmed, filtered and redistributed, slightly purified, to the users;
or dumped untreated in the sea. There are some small-scale local systems
that deserve further study, if time permits. *[Appendix 27b, Sewage Treatment]*.

Other species who share the planet simply void their waste to rot into the ground.
Certain species, called pets, are kept with affection by humans, who walk around
with them attached to cables, and carefully scoop their poop (pet name for shit)
[Appendix 33, ibid] into hoarded plastic baggies which they tie up and deposit
into dedicated receptacles, which are later emptied into bigger bags and bins
and transported to vast containers. I have yet to learn where this procedure ends.

There is an industry around ordure (shit) and manure (rotted shit). They bag it
in the ubiquitous plastic, and sell it to each other to spread on the dirt
where they want to grow more food, so they don't have to consume their own shit.

Example 2

Chemical, industrial and nuclear waste, which may yet prove fatal to the Earth.

[continued]

Bellyful

From the foul carcass I begin
to pick off the remains of flesh,
the shreds drying at the edges,
still moist around the absent bones.
I throw the spiky skeleton out
to the famished gulls and dogs.
The men will return soon,
sharp-set from their skirmishes,
so I focus on this skinny mess,
start its transformation,
through the alchemy of rue and vinegar,
into something they will devour
without thought, and belch into sleep.
In a few hours I must find another way
to gratify their curdled appetites.
Tomorrow I will go mushrooming.

Extinction

The waterline is hesitant and hidden
beneath a weight of weed,
a mass moved by unsudden
undulations. In one direction the sea,
in the other immobile, impossible
beach, bearing dried cities of tangle,
shelters hollowed into habitable
greenish grottos, spangled
with plastic particles and broken glass,
in which we survive the onslaught,
weaving hope from the horizon and seagrass,
carefully carrying sun-distilled water
poured from our palms into close-woven
baskets, before the sweetness seeps
away. Always we accost the ocean,
invisible under the invasion of ropes
and rafts of seaweed, suffocating slowly
any life persisting through the plague.
Occasionally over the surface wholly
blanketed and bound, a vague
bristling of the permeant pelt
moves and mounts into the reek,
till it tears open, tilts to a halt,
revealing empty eye-sockets, teeth
shiv-sharp, overgrown, underused,
famished fish of the deep braving
the surface to search for food. Eyeless, confused,
aware of alien air minimally moving,
the great heads swerve and swing
from side to side, sampling the atmosphere.
Blind, unblinking, blowing and snapping,
they sink back into what was once their
habitat, to hang in stagnant brine, viscid
with the ripped remains of lesser fish.
Filleted bones carpet the coral bed,
incremental light illumines crushed
shells, shattered caves, the startling shine
of bioluminescence, borne through confusion
by abysmal anglerfish, among myriads of marine
creatures, all coming to a natural conclusion.

Stone Circles

Afterwards the animals did well,
there was a lot of available flesh
for a while,
and for a while it was quickly refreshed
by not-quite-survivors, who fatally fell
where they stood
and where they stood became a stench
even the beasts couldn't bear to smell,
even for food.

The full effects were hidden at first.
They turned on each other and fed
for a while,
and for a while a few were led
by killer instincts, unquenchable thirst
for blood.
For blood there was until it reversed;
such desiccated bodies were no good,
even for food.

The brave and desperate nosed the piles
of debris, pawed them cautiously and licked
for a while
and for a while ingesting made them sick.
Hunger evolved, took pebbles and nails
even, for food.
They hacked and heaved, regurgitated sticks,
ate them again and again, they couldn't fail,
they understood

they had to eat what earth provides.
Not much was left of plenty, gone
for a while.
For a while they broke their teeth on stone,
swallowed bits of metal, died

where they stood.
But some still stood, determined, tried
and died again, until it changed for one,
and rotting wood

became the first food to sustain
their lives. Then rock and rusted metal followed
for a while
and for a while tortured each swallow.
Survival – synonym for pain –
even for food.
They survived, and for their lives regained
they made stones sacred, ringed and hallowed
where they stood.

Verisimilitude

An anthracite sky
is not the same as
a solid sky made of anthracite,
spitting teeth
over a bulldozed landscape.

Flames flicker in puddles of oil,
generators of their own supine rainbows,
because the sun is hidden
behind opaque formations.
Simulacrums of cumulus and raindrops
ricochet off pockmarked rocks,
mute and toothless on the edge
of extinction.
    Think of it.
    Extinction of rocks,
battered and pounded
into acrid ground
by proliferations of sky-stones,
clattering a pebbled beach
on a random strand of space.

Fortune Swallower

The tricks are learned from early childhood watching
or sometimes being the hapless assistant
obliged to lend sweat or tears to the mix.

The best days involve changing someone's ill-fortune
pulling a hair, wrapping it round a skin-tag
till it falls away starved of bad luck.

Mostly boredom fills the week –
baking fingernails into a cake
tearing a cuticle till it bleeds
and drops into the fermented porridge
licking lips, not necessarily yours.

The smells cling, you live in a miasma.
The air howls silently with the extractions,
swallowing triggers a gagging reflex.

Your gut reactions are seldom gentle.

Glosa on 'Terra Incognita', by Helen Dunmore: *Inside the Wave*

Or the first touch of untouched terrain
On our footsoles, as the land explores us,
Have become our fortune. Let me explain
Which foods are good to eat, and which poison.

There's joy in returning to a loved location
to walk beside our younger ghosts for company
to see with unshortened eyes the importance
of things blurred from distance and foreground.
Not without melancholy, to note the changes wrought
by time, to weave a pavement again and again
checking where a lost facade once moved past
with a familiar nod of reflection or foliage,
where sounds reacted thus; now absence or pain,
or the first touch of untouched terrain

itself becomes familiar to all the senses,
if our presence prevails, repeats, responds,
pores over the new surfaces and angles, or turns
to past and future, hurries onward in search, research
of what seemed, but never was, stable. The world,
like bodies, constantly renews, without fuss.
This corner crumbles slowly and is gone
to the vine feeling its way picturesquely through
cracked balustrades, moving earth till there is less
on our footsoles as the land explores us

while we think we explore the land. Looking for
somewhere to put down roots, we root out
whatever's hard or in the way. Sometimes
minerals, or gems, or fossilised riches. We find
we stand on something, call it ours, a home
sweet home, embroider the indifferent refrain
to hang on walls and think about in hardship,

as soldiers dug into their quagmired shelters,
or travellers beating through the alien grain
have become our fortune. Let me explain.

We stay at home, we think shielded from harm,
construct our bubbles, all catered needs within,
watch horror fiction for our entertainment
and horror fact through HD digital glass.
The harsh world, barely tamed, swirls just beyond,
domain of soldiers, travellers, all folk who have reason
fondly to caress the fictional embroidery, to dream
a place of safety, but keep us all alive by keener need
to learn the hidden land, the offers of each season,
which foods are good to eat, and which poison.

Beyond Belief

Blue ballistic beetles buzz,
wings blinged and beautiful.
At random intervals one bursts –
with soft, harmonious boom!
A little mist brimful of jewels
hovers and blows away.

Bedecked in polychrome plumage, birds
bob on the forest floor.
Silk-full spiders and beady-bugs run
between them to see the show.
Gaudy butterflies fluttering by,
pause out of boredom to perch

on the balconies of trees to watch
the battle beginning below –
brutal beating of earth by wings,
bewailing the harsh beloved,
the broken heart, but... beauty turns,
bestows her favour, bonds.

Bombastic, brilliant blowfish mouth
impressive embouchure,
blowing bassoons with bubbling ease,
their tootling gurgles along
under the ocean, over the waves,
swims far beyond belief.

Hot Wind

(Zizi Jeanmaire in Khartoum)

She blows in to Al Mogram Park
by the Nile's blue white
rond de jambe from source to sea,
flashes her wide mouth,
pointes in the scuffed dust.
A crowd forms around her
softness uncovered
urchin crop:
> *grande révérence...*

Thunder might be memories,
violence impressed on the air,
horse hooves, camel feet, the future
of the present gathering a crowd
as yet only intrigued,
> *petit jeté battu, fouetté.*

Saharan winds suck lips, eyes, skin.
Slow orange wall chokes airways.
Brisé. The crowd melts
away. *Khamsin* juggernauts
over the city closed inside
> *haboob, simoom.*

Chassé, battement, grand jeté,
Zizi leaps glittering among mica
flecks in near-solid air.
Heat handles her body
shivers like feathers,
like sand plumes tease a crowd
lip-slicking its thirst.
She slants into the storm,
> *effacée.* Curtain.

Fidel Castro in the Cold

The beard will keep your chin warm
but take care in the hot springs.
So said Mama Castro,
wrapping a muffler round his neck.

Oh too hot Mama!
he said gently removing the scarf
before it soaked with sweat.

Fidel blew her a kiss from the top
of the stairs and disappeared into the Ilyushin.
His mother watched it taxi,
dabbing discreetly at her eyes.

She was right of course about the springs.
So happy at the thought of being warm
again in Iceland's sharpened winter
he plunged –
                          leapt out a scalded cat,
water boiling in his beard,
wrung out too late not to flay
his face, peel away
his hail-fellow-well-met persona.

Blistered beneath his facial hair
he thundered back to Cuba,
unlit Havana clenched
between his teeth.

The Trade Commissioner from the 5th Moon Considers his Prospects

My posterior eyes check the intricate Insignia of Office on my back.
My lateral eyes admire my four impressive golden epaulettes.
I flick the cuffs of my sleeves. The silk runs gratifyingly up my four arms,
whispers over the macula of eyeballs rising and falling through my skin.
The exo-tracery of lymph and blood vessels forms a lovely lace upon my hands.

Are my digits beginning to look old, in spite of their immaculate ungual grooming?
I flex them individually and note the unrestricted movement, the pleasing pliability
so successfully applied to and from my gender specific partners (I always insist on this,
allowing a range of definitions over an alphabet of active nights). The tips tingle
in anticipatory pleasure. I am sure my hosts will provide the requisite playmates.

I raise my appraisal to the room around me and decide I am satisfied.
I have been given an appropriately hefty suite in seven-star accommodation.
There will be no problem fitting my many muscular limbs in the bed, nor a companion,
and I will be able to watch my progress in the cherub-embellished ceiling mirror,
which no doubt hides a plethora of spy-cams and recorders. I shall perform for them.

It is good to know tomorrow I will be provided with an escort of honour, crowds
with placards and message balloons will line the route to the Senate on the lake.
I will be fawned over by representatives of this planet and its many satellites.
These smiling idiots think they know what I want but none of them can guess
at the exhaustive range of my appetite for Life. I lick some of my lips.

Mash up

Tiger lilies roar so loud
the goose grass flies away,
the clever fox glove stands so proud,
horse radish rears and neighs.

Spider plants run up the wall,
thin snake beans slither fast,
crab apples run diagonals,
cow parsley ambles past.

Dog daisies whine and bark and howl
and catkins dance and tap,
henbane lays a golden shell,
the elephants' ears flap.

Duck weed leaves the mucky pond
to dive into sea grape
and bay leaves in the blue beyond,
while elder berries gape.

In haste witch hazel flaps and whoosh –
flies off without a broom,
crashes into the butterfly bush,
which flutters to its doom.

Buttercups and snowdrops melt
away without a sound
but everything is boogieing
with life, just underground.

Reproductive Practices of the *Psittocoid*

Puberty is triggered by the opening of the seventh eye
with which *Psittocoids* recognize the geometries,
finding certain curves and angles pleasing.

When this recognition becomes painful, they apply
for digital therapy to the edge of their tentacles,
        provided by immigrants from the third moon,
        whose eyeless expressions they cannot read.

                The results are docketed and stored in ice flasks,
                against the day when they make their choice.

When all ten eyes are open and everything blazes
with promise, they repeatedly circle the array of possibility
and judder to a halt beside a chosen extension;
vibration gradually melds them at the base of the first tentacle.

This is a time of unbridled carelessness,
when suckers and pores deliver fluids and noise
on a scale they find necessarily fulfilling
but many others hate.

After the third cycle of the furthest moon, comes
the Ceremony of the Ice Flask,
presented by each to the other
and melted against and into the scalding *psittocotic* gland.

Psittosacs under the now-withering first tentacle swell and break away.

        The sacs are given over to immigrants to lick and regurgitate,
        which keeps the temperature steady   until the contents explode
        over their hosts whom they devour,
        doubling in size with each revolution.

Meanwhile the parent bodies deplete and decline,
residual tentacles wither away,
all eyes turn inward, occlude and terminally close,
just before the progeny find them
comestible.

To Autumn

(with apologies to Keats)

O clammy fog! When will it lift?
This rotting fruit brings bees and wasps.
I can't enjoy a drink outside
without them there to share my cup –
anaphylaxis! Scary.

The angle of sun and shadow shifts,
bogs me down, makes me depressed.
S.A.D. raises its ugly head.
The only way out of it is sleep,
drugged if necessary.

Spring is so far, I feel bereft,
must weather fall and winter first.
I wish I could follow the swallows' lead,
fly south over a brightening map,
alight, warm and weary.

Locked in

I am honeyed in
amber transparency
splayed for examination
of substance and freighted contents.

Double lenses cluster round
peering into my immobility
mouthing cold questions
I can't answer.

Once I could stretch my legs,
bask in knowledge of my wings,
revel in the syncopated facets
of my compound visions.

Now I can't
vibrate, feed,
breed or hum;
my gleam
halted
by the resin
that trapped
my flight.

Nox Longa

She became conscious of penumbra,
smelled a presence sucking
nausea through the wound to wrack her
body with spasms of distress.
She depleted with each seizure,
until nurses took her slowly up the ward
into a side-room to unveil her cries,
stupefy her with syringes of time being.
Her echoes cycled through degrees of fear,
bristled the night watch air, thickened breath.

Then it came snuffling between the beds,
dragging, it seemed, a heavy thing behind.
Its protean shadow climbed and contracted
across my half-drawn curtains, brushing air
into a sough of menace: nearer, further, nearer.
My heart beat down all other sound, held me
petrified within my own engulfing dread.
Black slipped off the screen, gathered
darkness, encompassed the vacant bed,
settled its patient vigil on her possible return.

Doffed

When the bad news came
he dusted off his fedora,
flicked the brim
over his forehead
and strolled to his favourite café.
He watched the world continue
to talk and yell and laugh
as if all the tales were true.

He became recognisable
by his sharp suit and hat,
always at the same table,
chatting about this and that,
small, cheerful banter
worn, like his snappy suit,
over a dodgy centre;
cool hat over tough shit.
When he needed help to walk
he carefully chose a cane,
eccentric accent to the craic,
to thump and point and thump again.

In the hospice he went cigaretted,
with shades and a bright red robe,
to sit outside, always black-hatted,
on a bench on the public road.

Till he doffed it, lay back on the pillows
exhausted. Closed eyes,
chest bellows and morphine,
uncovered
the last few days.

Archaeology

She's an old lady now,
she's folded her nipples away,
locked up unseemly lust
in an intricate antique box,
with newspaper clippings, locks
of polychromatic hair
and the arrogance of youth.

Gossip may pop the catch
in a cloud of allergens.
People will poke and scratch
at scabs on the remains.
When everything's laid bare,
time's ambiguous dust
will settle upon the truth.

Fairground

Old age is a malicious hall of mirrors
where I and all my loved ones curve and bend.
I watch our features candlewax in horror,
to puddle in this vicious hall of mirrors,
misshapen, morphed, disabled by our sorrows,
in warped reflections on the place hope ends –
old age. It's a malicious hall of mirrors
where I and all my loved ones curve and bend.

the last syllable

— self portrait as crow —

old grey crow with crooked wing leans
her comedy into the window recess
enjoys a zephyr plumage-messing
splaying the deep blue black
playing over her back
before it blows the scene

her eye opens scans for the next one
rippling trees in that direction
here it comes she opens her beak
swallows the ticklish air croaks
in pleasure step changes claw to claw
shivers uneven wings for more

takes off in falling fashion
ungainly into gainly flight
not much left but feather-fustian
and the questionable joy of far far sight
clear peering into future and past
the ever-present present cannot last
but makes good company follows
with petty pace tomorrow and tomorrow and tomorrow

The old neighbourhood

I can't name the city now, it's gone
into a different map. Bombay, Mumbai,
city of hanging gardens bubble-wrapped
around me, packed in a camphor chest.

This was once just rough terrain
before the houses, new buildings
more roads, a flyover, an underpass.
The new geography is strange to me.

the cliff still falls away to the right

Now at Gamadia Road, turn left,
follow the flyover heading south,
look over the edge at Kemps Corner
for yesterday…

There is the Kemps Corner Hotel.
I never knew Leonard Cohen
stayed there in search of enlightenment.
I would have joined the search.

the cliff falls away to the right

Today I uncover the city in my head,
ocean broken on the sea wall,
where as a child I was carefully taken,
whether I wanted to be or not.

Now I do. I notice everything that isn't there:
The wild ground where lantana bushes grew,
the monsoon-stained villas, hutments,
the vulture-heavy palm trees, childhood.

the cliffs fall away

LIVE CANON